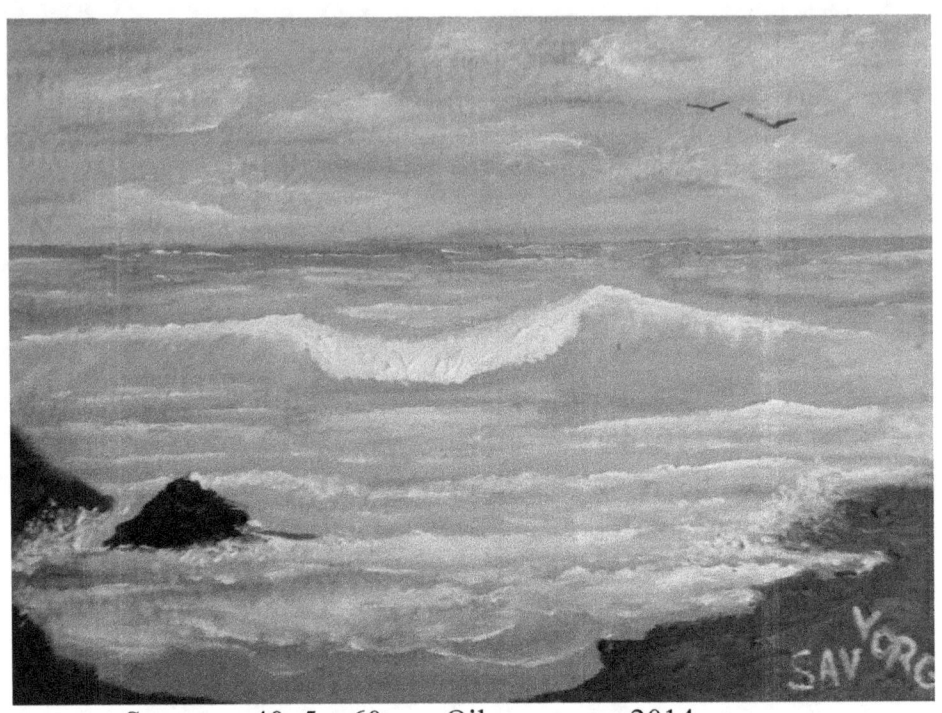

Sea wave 40. 5 x 60 sm. Oil on canvas 2014 year

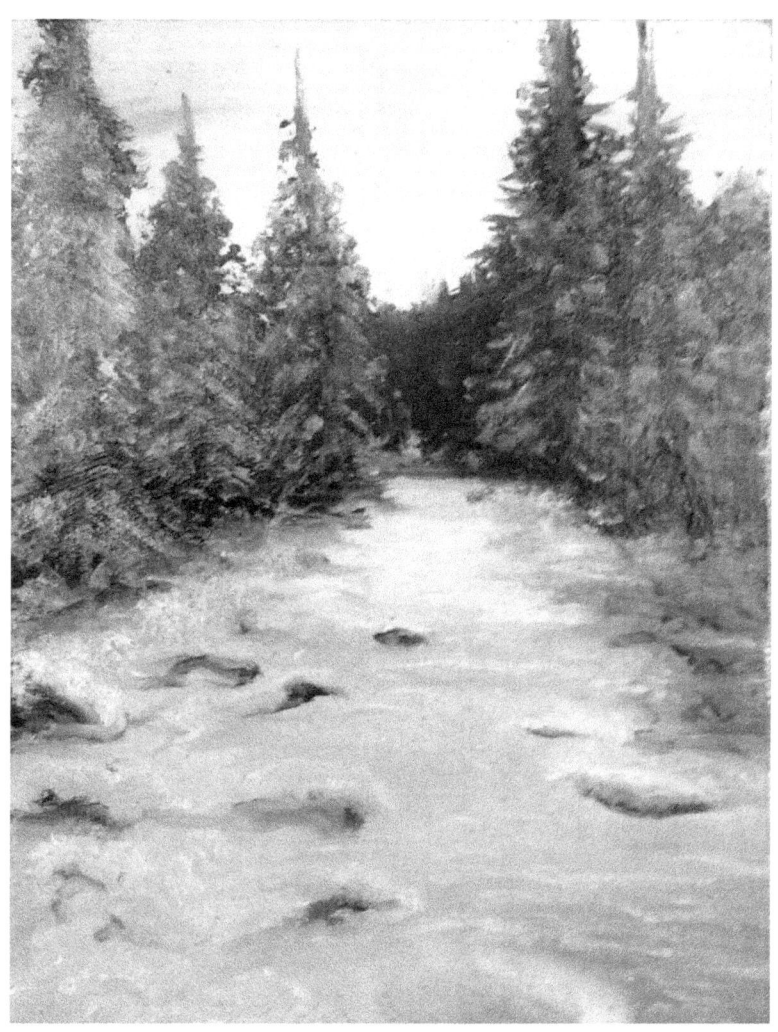

Winter river 25 x 39.5 sm. Oil on canvas

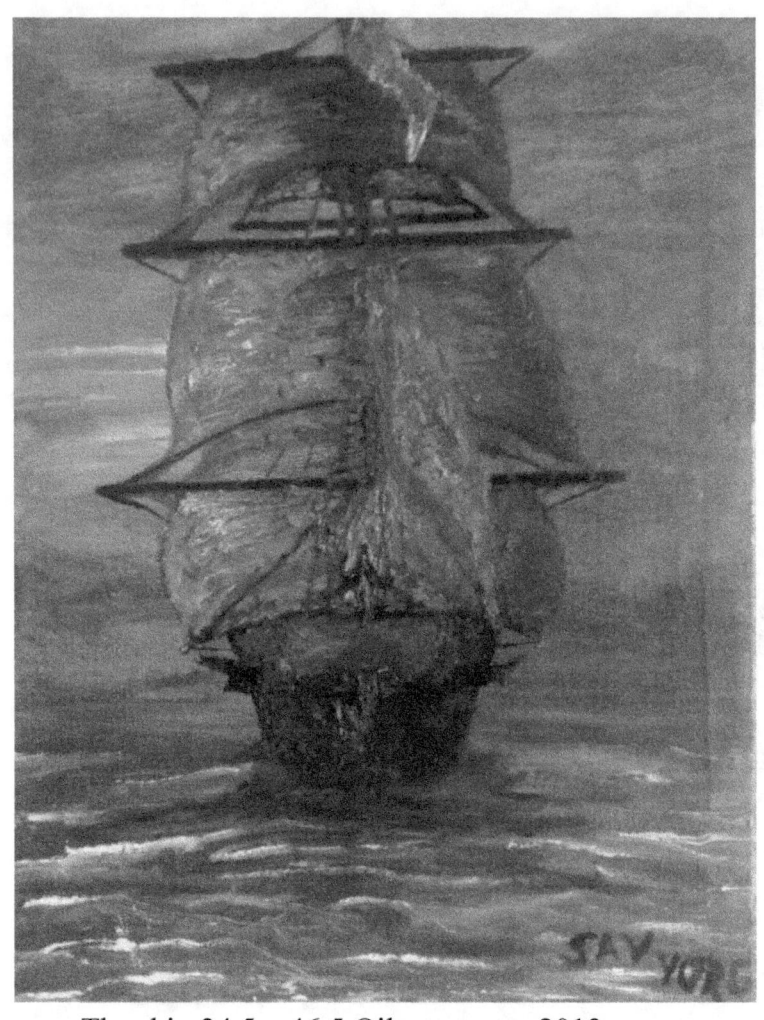

The ship 34.5 x 46.5 Oil on canvas 2013 year

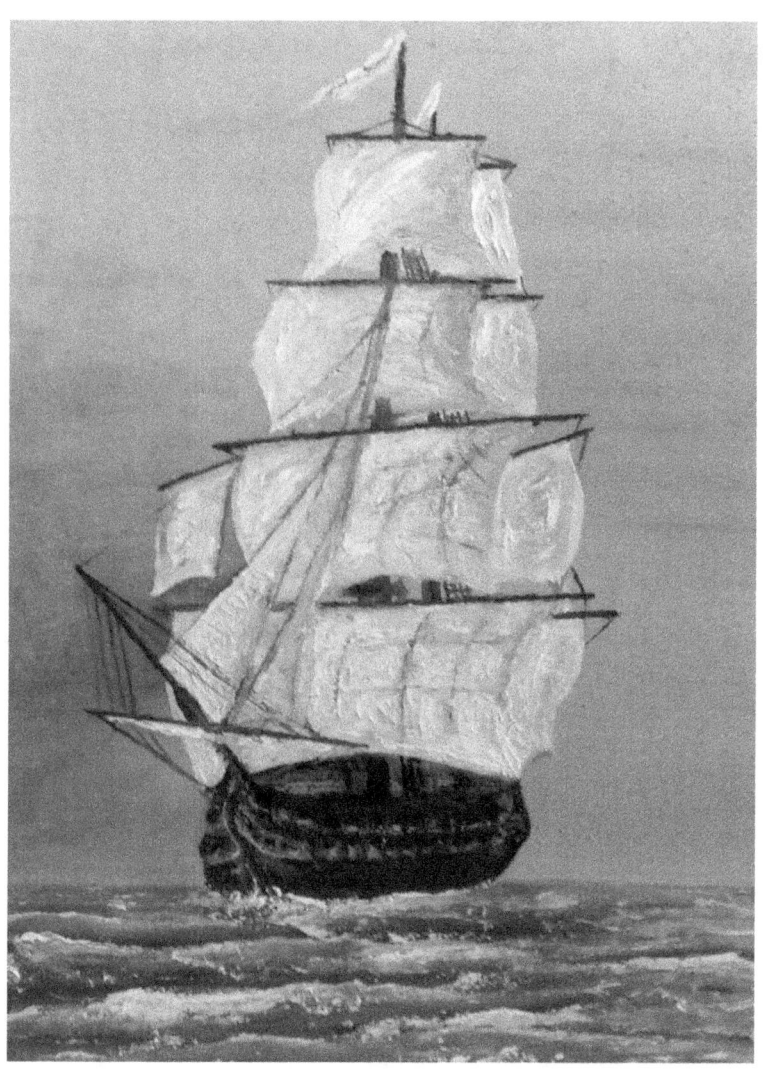

The ship 2   36 x 46.5 sm Oil on canvas. 2014 year

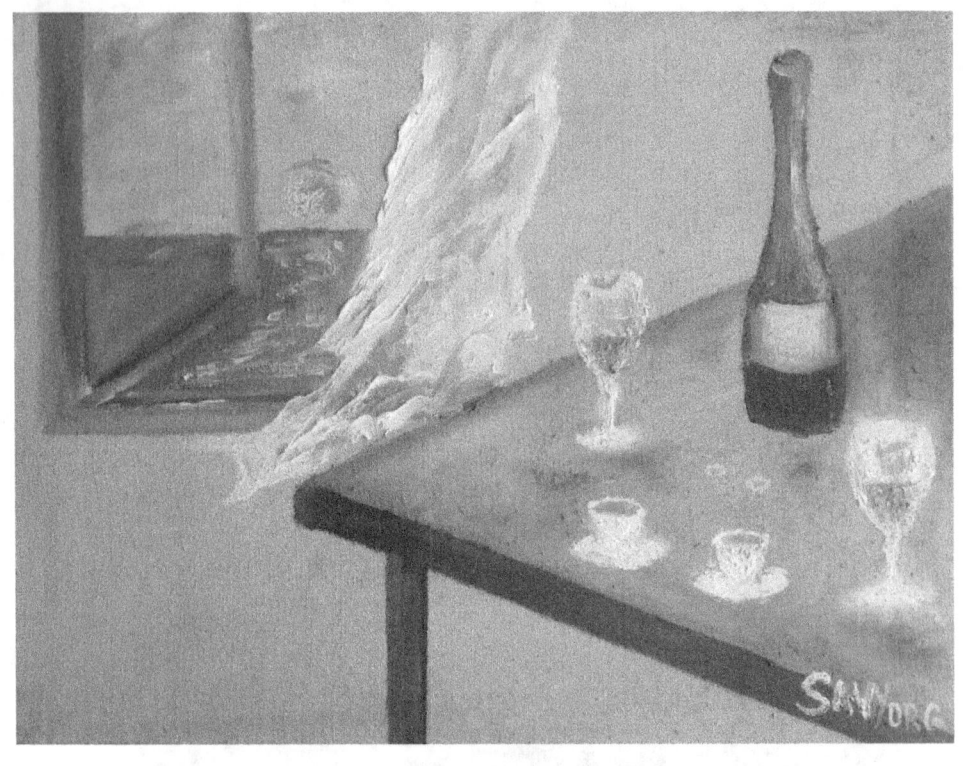

In the morning 37 x 46.5 sm. Oil on canvas 2014 year

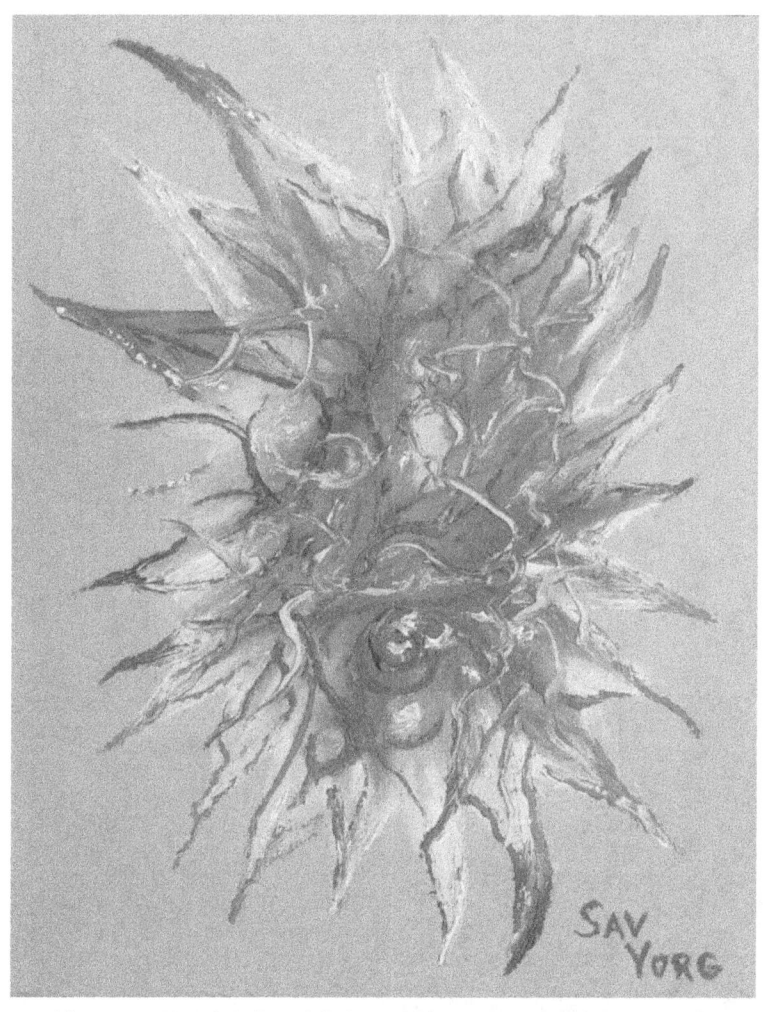

Abstract F a 34.5 x 46.5 sm. Il on canvas 2014 year

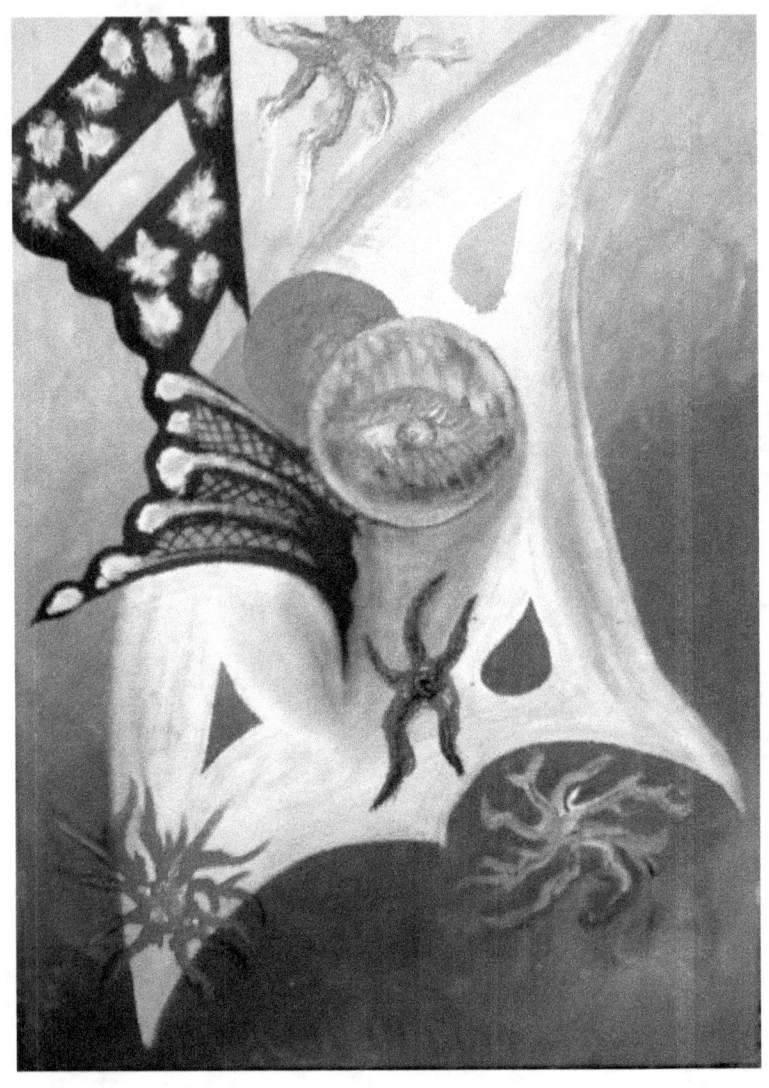

Abstract F b 38 x 58 sm. Oil on canvas 2008 year

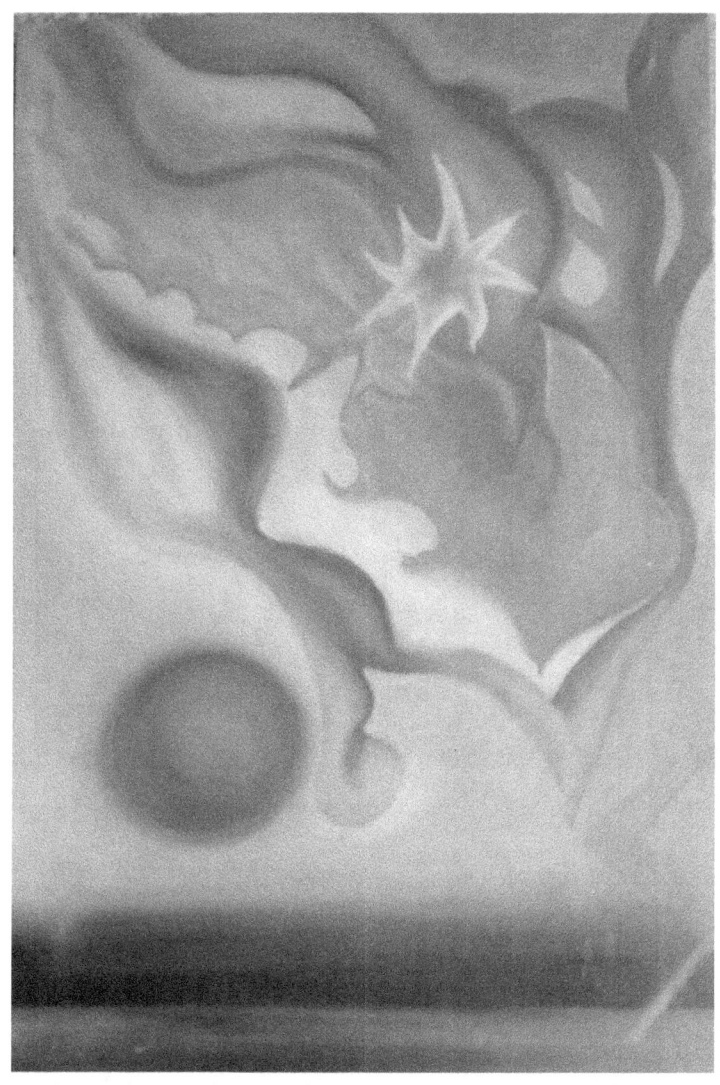

Abstract F c 39.5 x 60 sm. Oil on canvas 1988 year

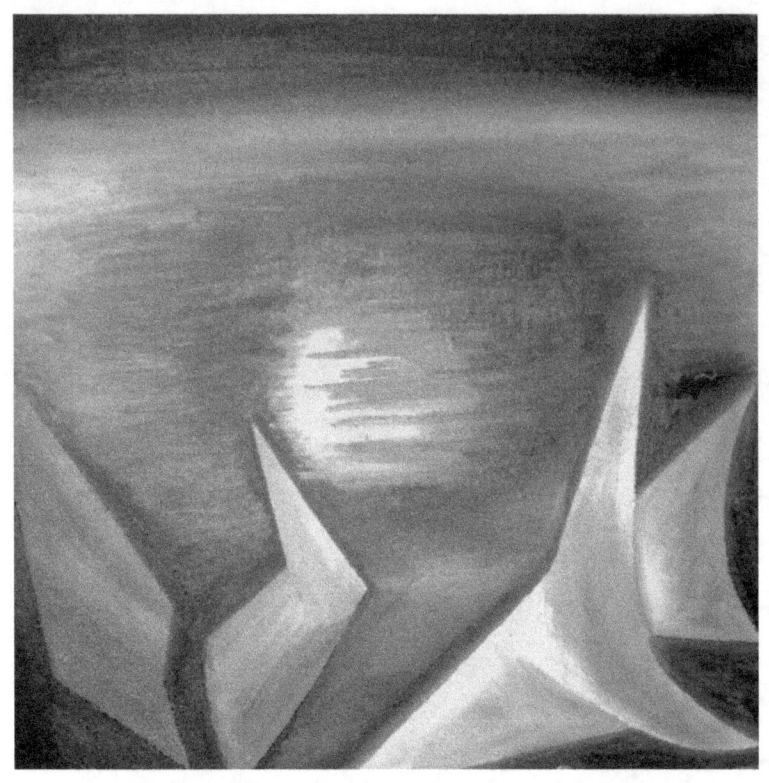

Abstract F d 50 x 50 sm. Oil on canvas 1989 year

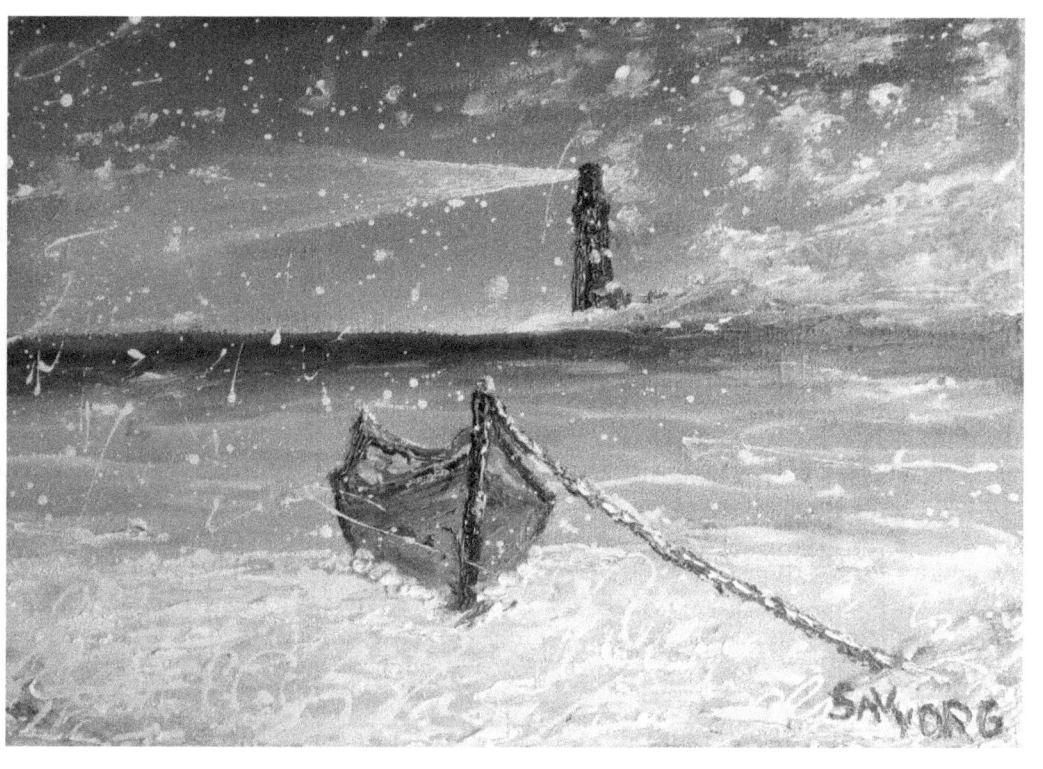

Winter Sea 37 x 52 Oil on canvas 2014 year

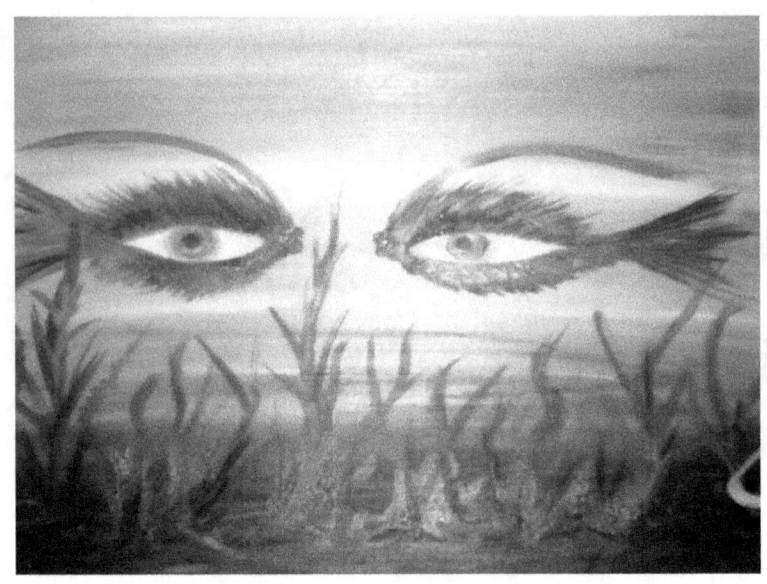

Two fish 41 x 30.5 sm. Oil on canvas 2005 year

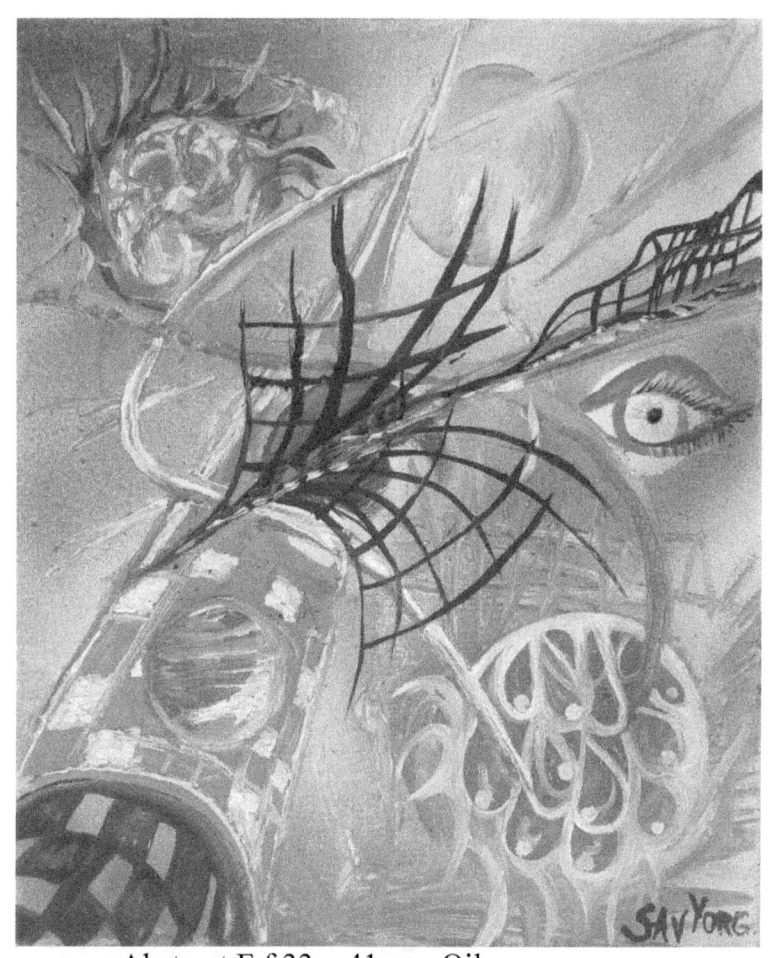

Abstract F f 33 x 41 sm. Oil on canvas

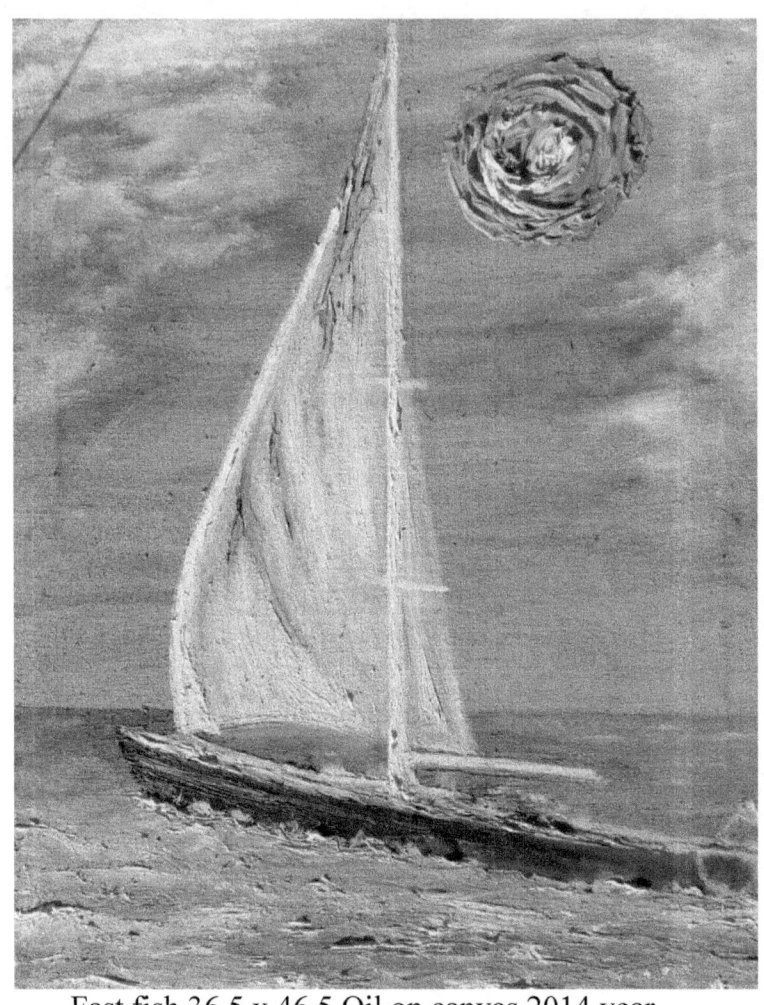

Fast fish 36.5 x 46.5 Oil on canvas 2014 year

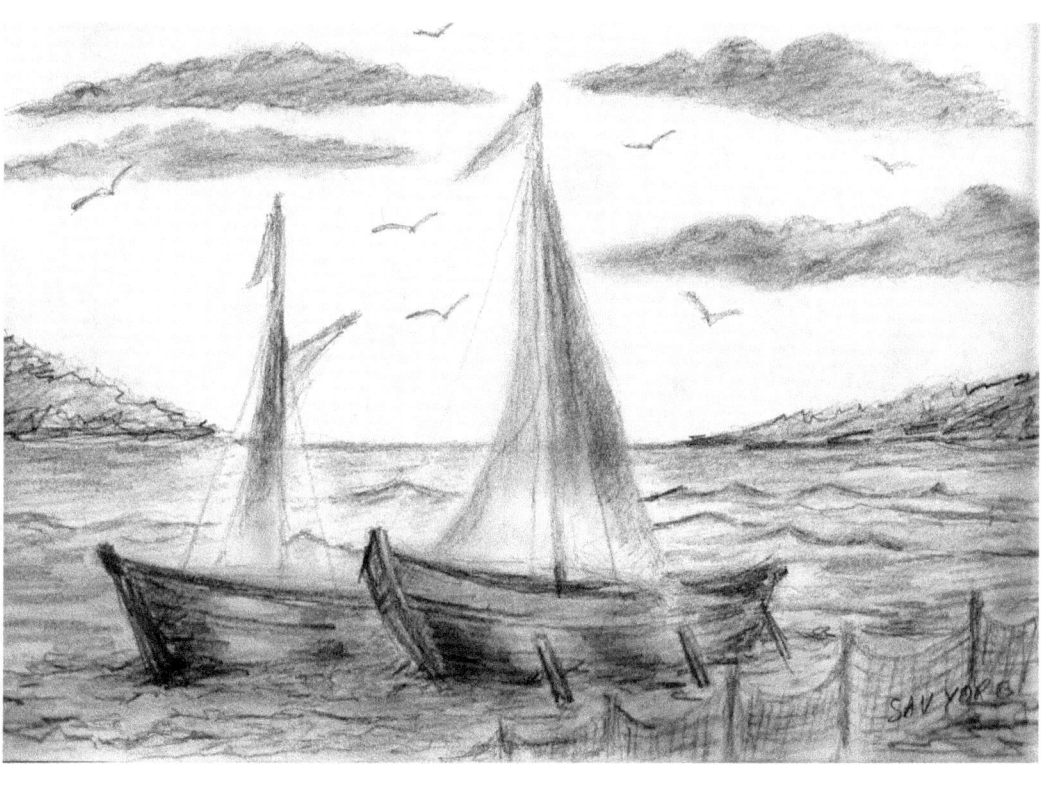

Two boats pencil drawing 2013 year 25 x 14 sm

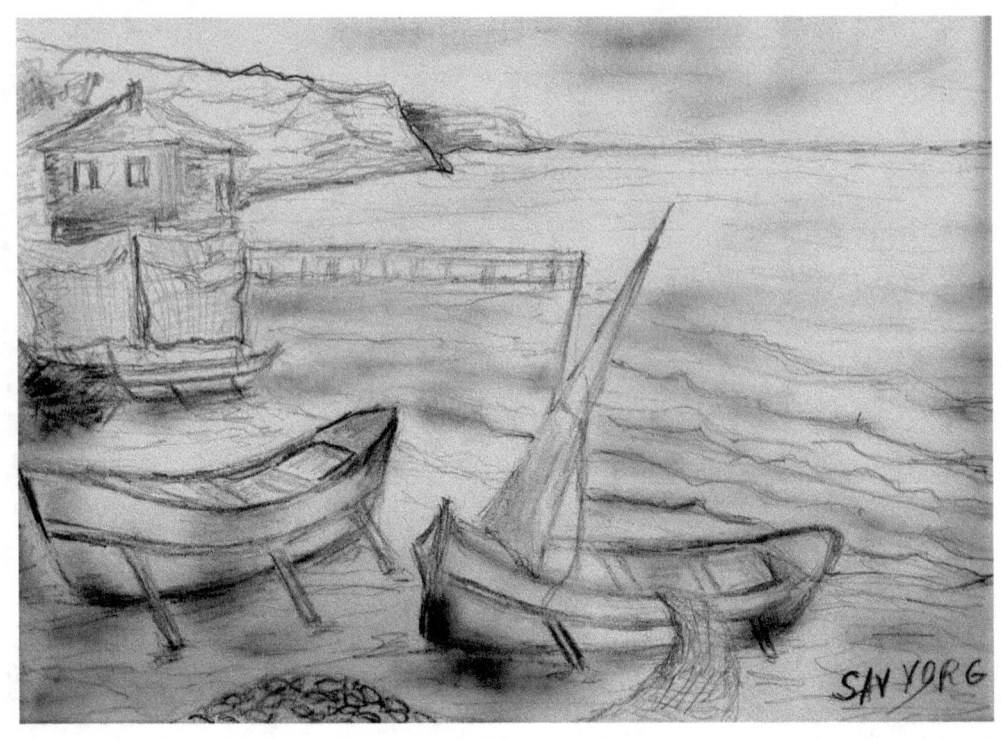

Graphic

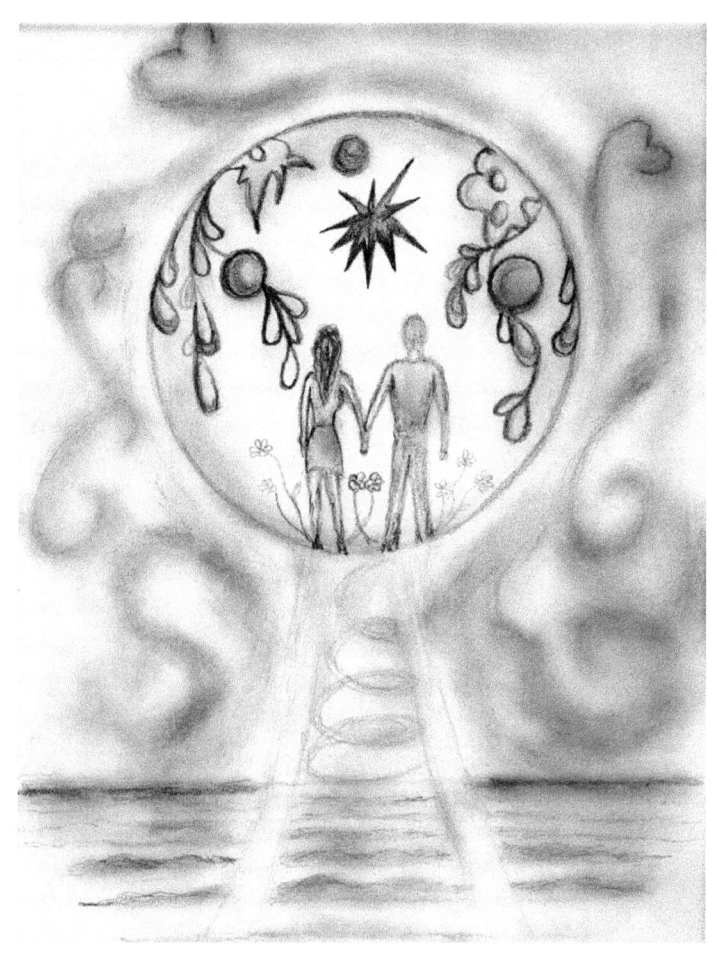

Graphic – Everlasting love

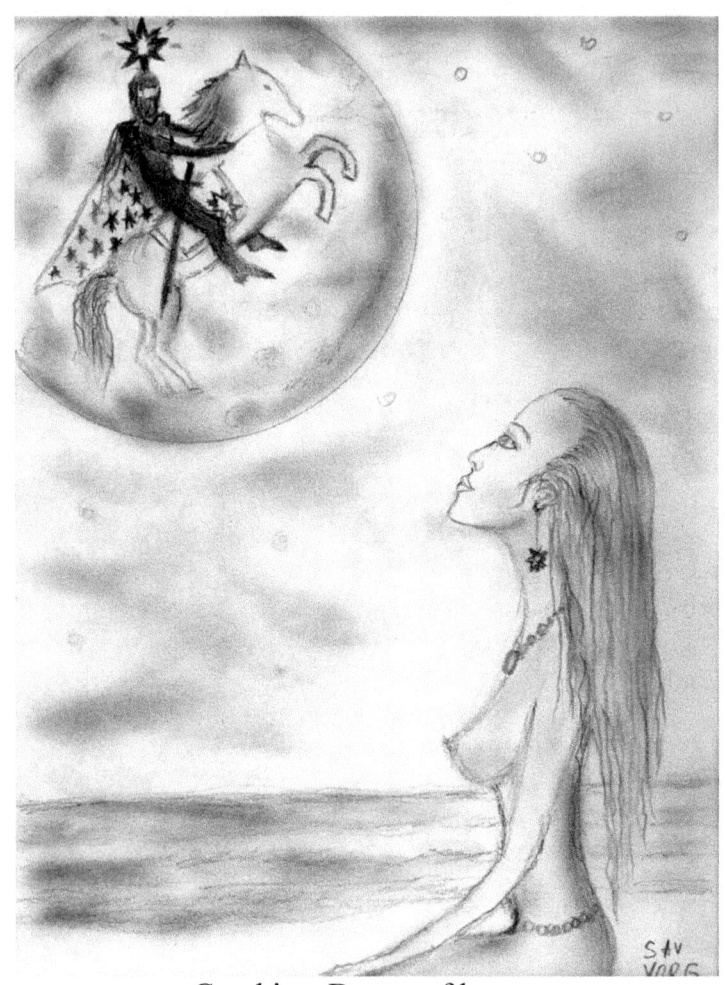

Graphic – Dream of love

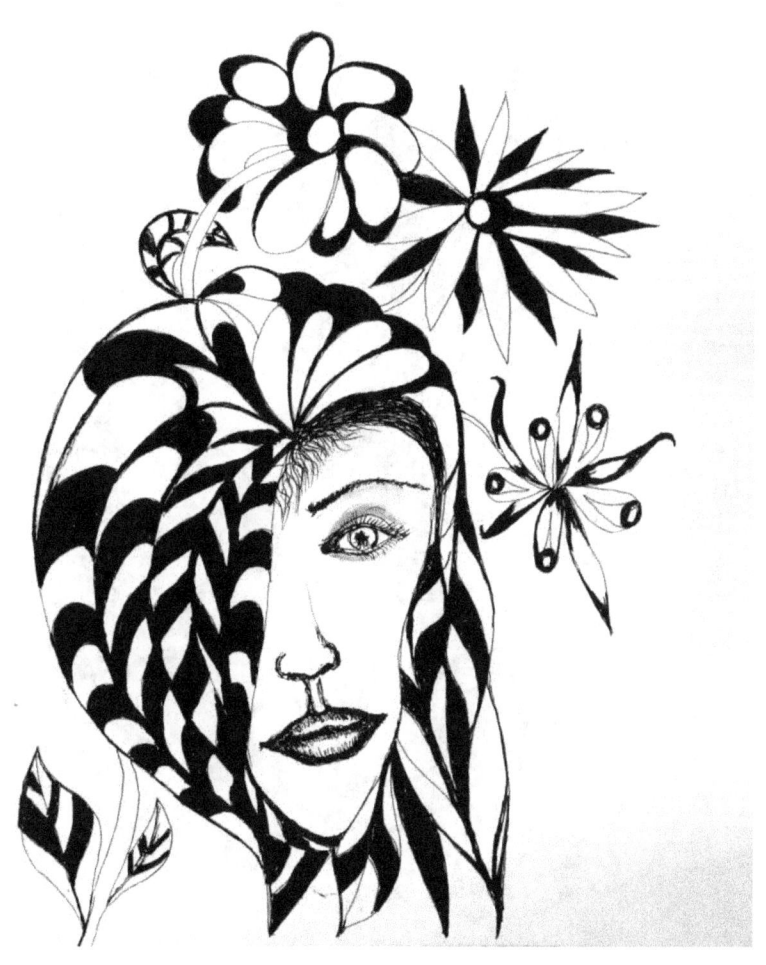

Girl flower graphic

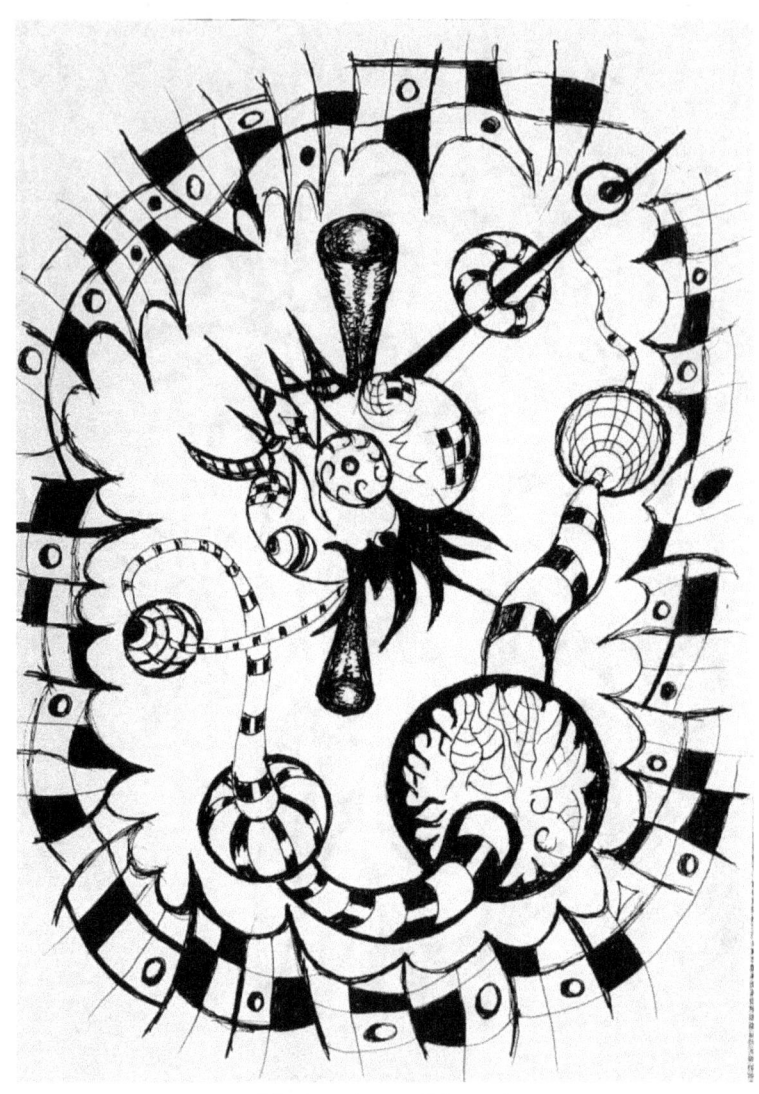

Abstract graphic

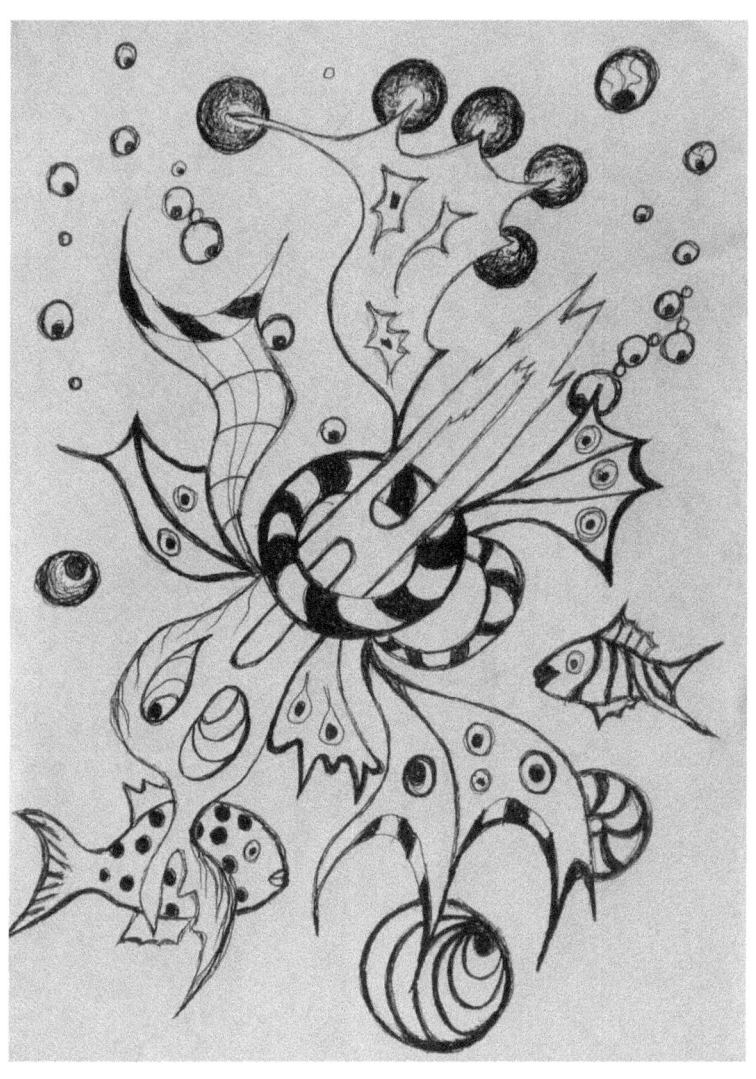

Abstract graphic – Sea world

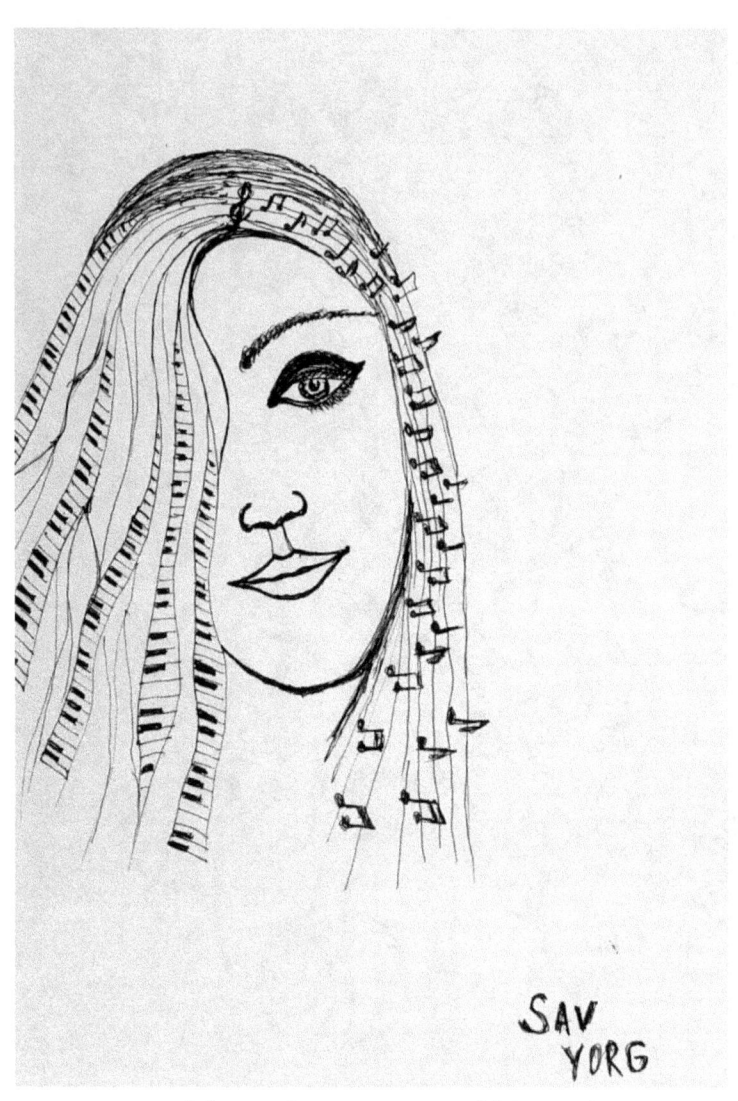

My music muse – graphic

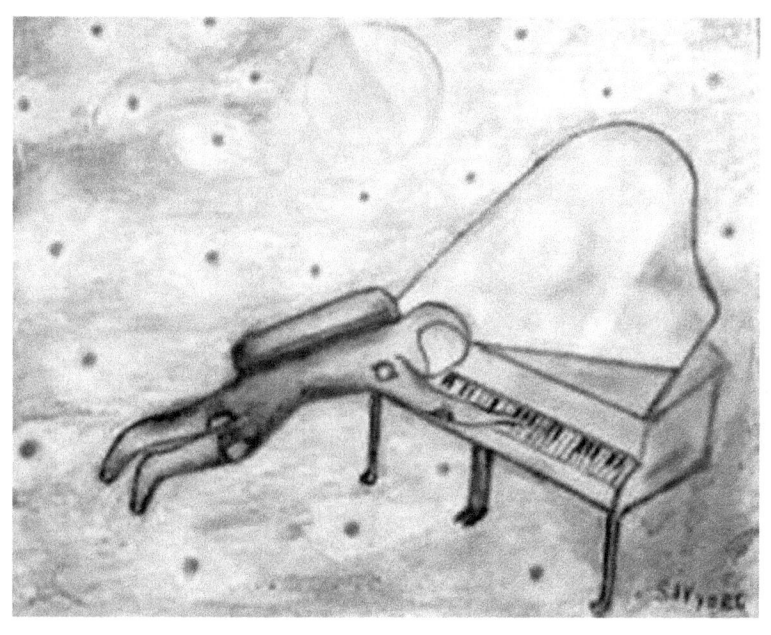

Passion for music – pastel

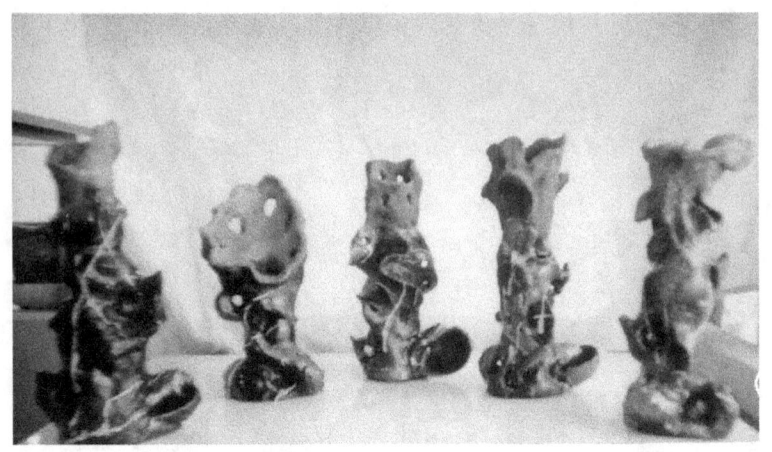

My vases – clay

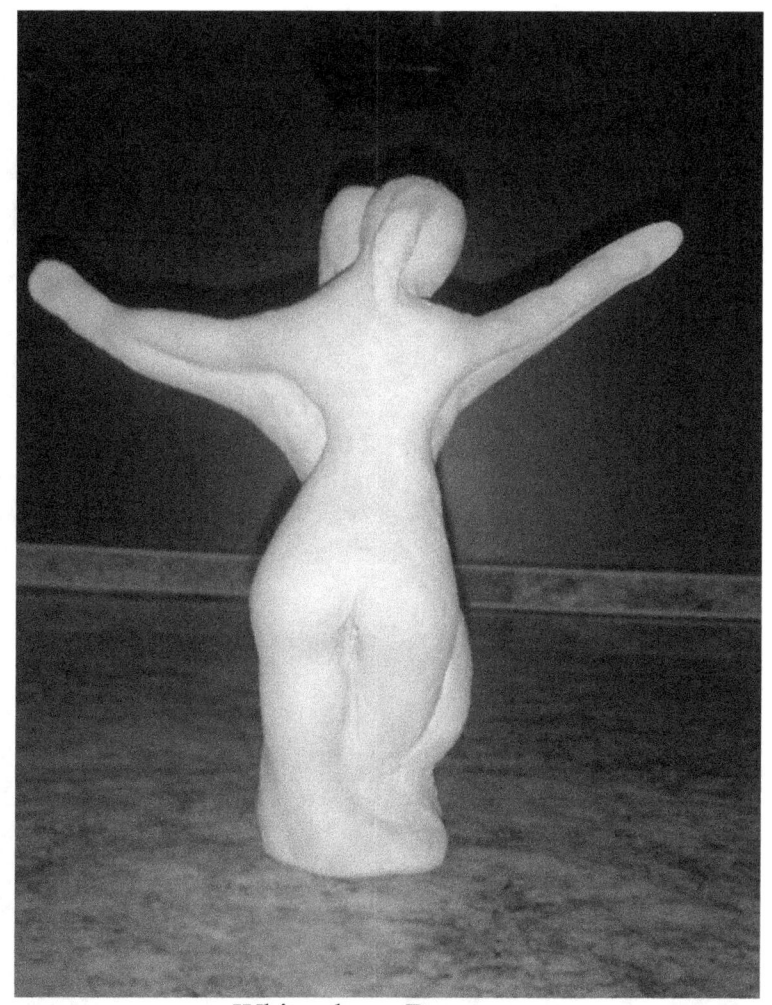

White clay – Dance

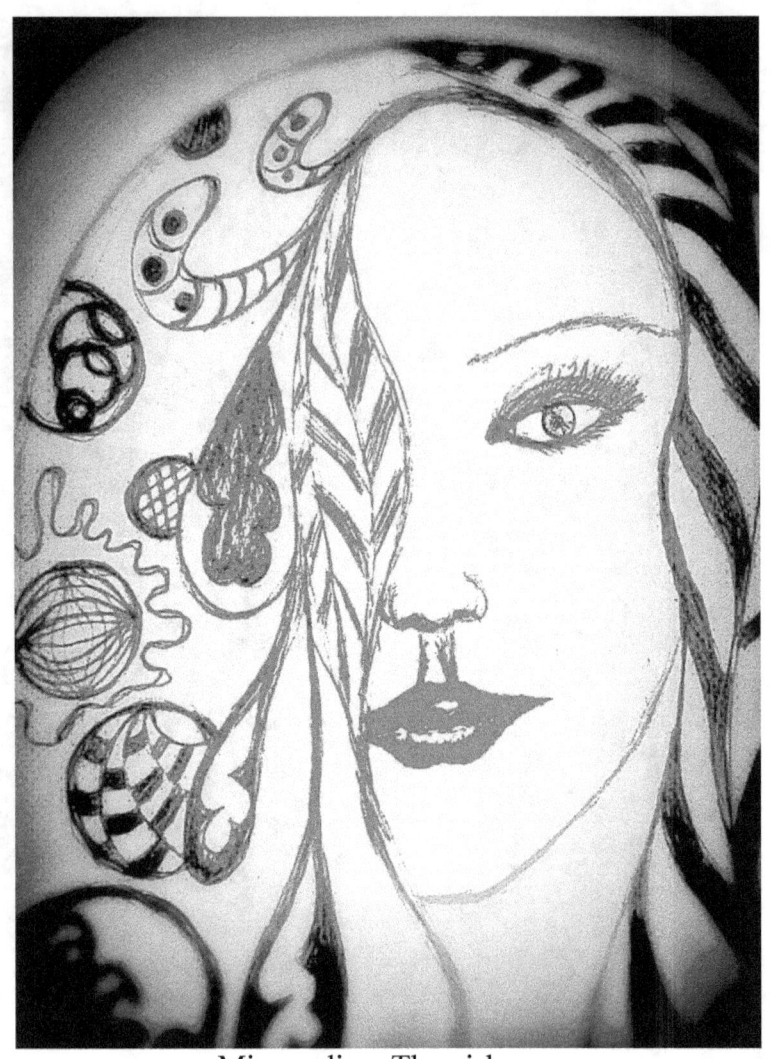

Mix media – The girl

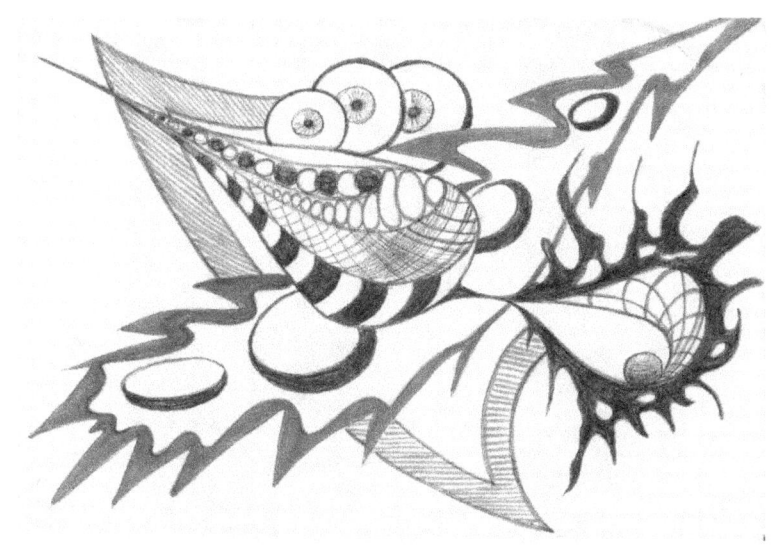

Abstract – mix media

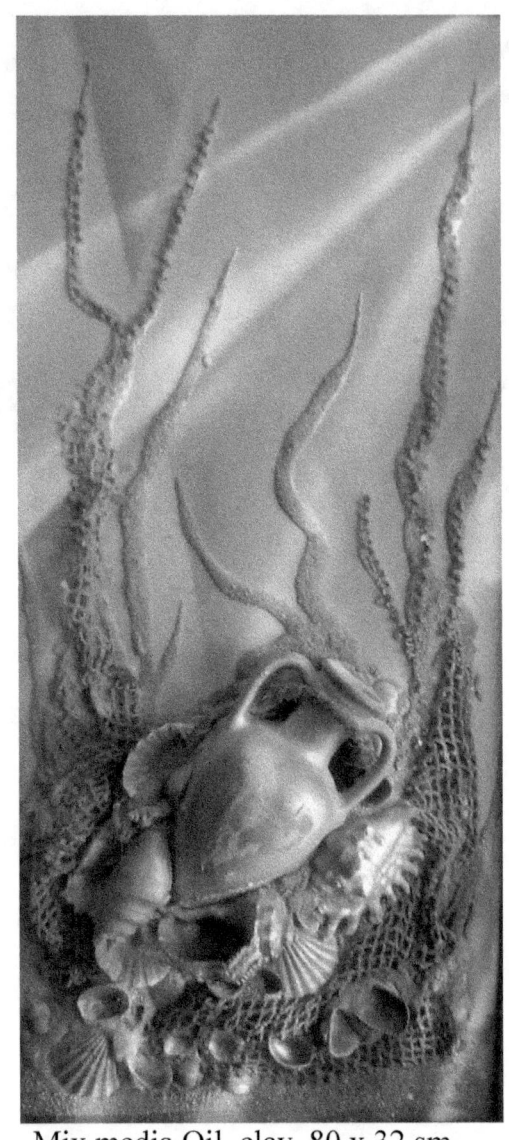

Mix media Oil, clay. 80 x 32 sm.

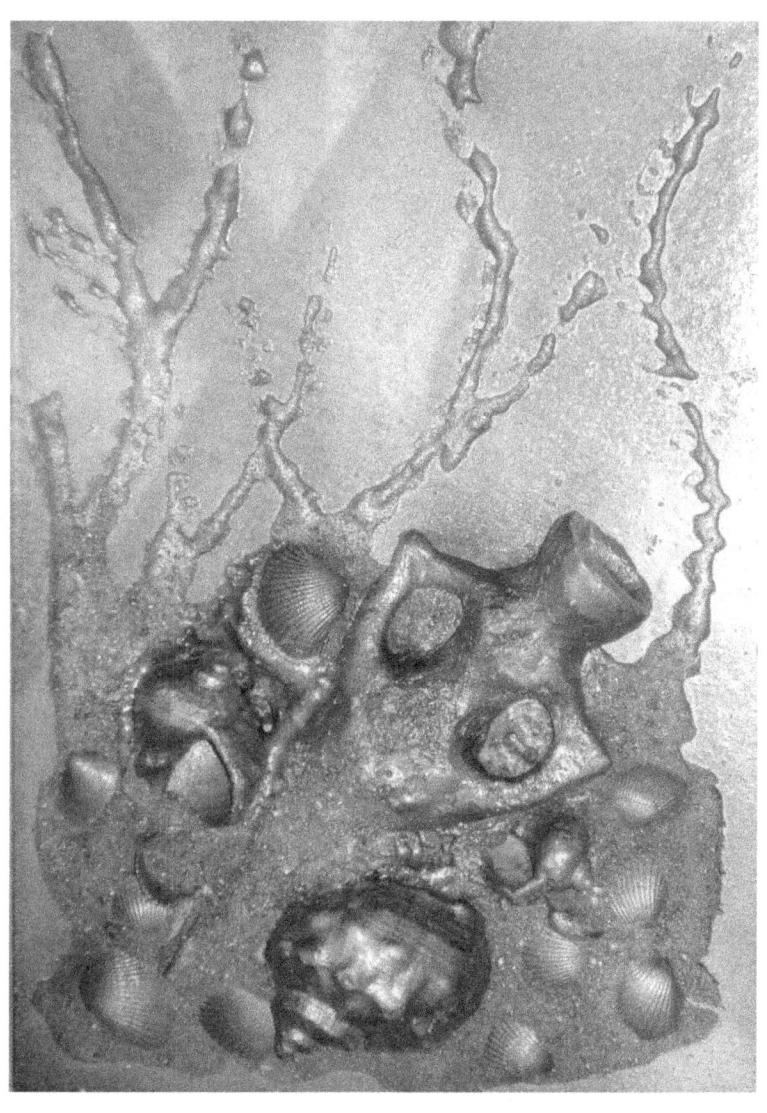

Mix media Oil, clay 42 x 25 sm

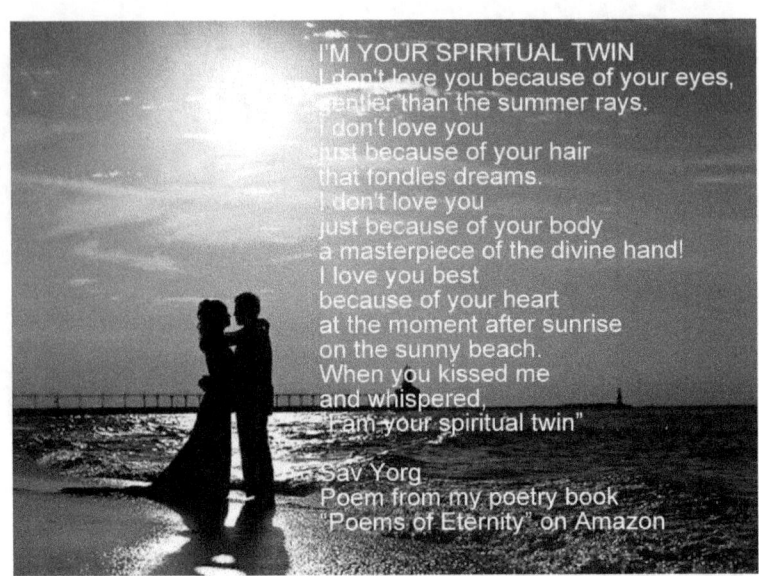

I'M YOUR SPIRITUAL TWIN
I don't love you because of your eyes,
gentler than the summer rays.
I don't love you
just because of your hair
that fondles dreams.
I don't love you
just because of your body
a masterpiece of the divine hand!
I love you best
because of your heart
at the moment after sunrise
on the sunny beach.
When you kissed me
and whispered,
"I am your spiritual twin"

Sav Yorg
Poem from my poetry book
"Poems of Eternity" on Amazon

Contact and orders E-mail unisav1@abv.bg
Original pictures and copies.
Art pal – sav11 gallery
print for a good price

www.ingramcontent.com/pod-product-compliance
Lightning Source LLC
Chambersburg PA
CBHW070730180526
45167CB00004B/1689